T0033478

ROLLIN' ON DOWN THE LINE

Lady Bird Johnson's 1964
Whistle-Stop Tour for Civil Rights

Written by Helen Kampion *and* Reneé Critcher Lyons

Illustrated by Erin McGuire

PUBLISHED *by* SLEEPING BEAR PRESS™

President Lyndon Baines Johnson (LBJ) picked up his pen while Dr. Martin Luther King Jr. and other civil rights leaders smiled over his shoulder. After years of struggle between Blacks and Whites, the president was signing the Civil Rights Act—a law declaring one citizen to be as equal as the next. Going forward, there would be no more separate drinking fountains, restaurant entrances, or even swimming pools for Black people.

LBJ knew some people in the South feared this law. But the president supported *all* Americans, even if it might cost him the upcoming November election, only four months away.

Lady Bird Johnson, the First Lady of the United States, knew someone needed to campaign and ask Southerners for their vote in the November election. Traveling to the South was too dangerous for the president—the Secret Service said so. Agents warned of riots, street fighting, and death threats.

But someone needed to step up; someone needed to explain why the new law was good for the country, and campaign for the president's re-election, too!

Lady Bird was the perfect person! Born in Texas, with family in Alabama, she belonged to the South, deep-rooted in Southern customs and traditions. She felt safe and at home there and would make the visit in support of the president and the Civil Rights Act.

As a child in Texas, Lady Bird had grown up with segregation. Blacks were forbidden to attend Whites-only schools and churches. Lady Bird wondered why her best friends could play with her in her front yard but not in the schoolyard.

She realized as a young girl, "This isn't right. Somebody ought to change this." Now the Civil Rights Act forced that change. Going from old customs to new ones wouldn't be easy. Campaigning with a Southern accent just might soothe hard feelings. The local crowds would recognize Lady Bird was "as much a part of the South as tobacco, peanuts, and red-eye gravy."

Yet American political wives had never campaigned alone. But that didn't stop Lady Bird. Neither did her fear of public speaking. Nor her husband's worry. Nor the Secret Service's warnings of possible danger.

Lady Bird insisted on visiting both friendly and unfriendly areas of the South as she and her all-lady staff planned a train tour. The press labeled the trip a whistle-stop tour since trains whistle over and over as they pass by or make stops. The train, named the Lady Bird Special, would whisk the First Lady and her staff through eight Southern states in four days.

Her decision to take action, "deeds, not words," as she described it, changed the role of the First Lady forever.

President Johnson and an estimated 10,000 other folks gathered at the train depot in **ALEXANDRIA, VIRGINIA**, for Lady Bird's send-off!

Bands played;

cameras snapped;

newsmen reported.

Lady Bird smiled, waved, and spoke to the eager crowd. "Sunshine and lots of friends—what could be a better way to start a whistle-stop? . . . I wanted to make this trip because . . . I am proud that I am part of the South. I love the South . . ."

"*Allllll* aboard the Lady Bird Special!" shouted the conductor.

During the twenty-minute ride to **FREDERICKSBURG, VIRGINIA**, where she would deliver her first speech of the tour, Lady Bird wrestled with mixed emotions. Although she looked forward to her trip, she still worried about the mood of the crowds and her speeches. She wanted to stress that Americans should "look for the ties that bind us together, not settle for the tensions that divide us."

As the train screeched into the station, Lady Bird walked to the open-air campaign car.

Supporters cheered; demonstrators booed; young men yelled, "Go home!"

Lady Bird did not flinch. . . . It was time to face Fredericksburg's protestors.

The First Lady's Southern drawl echoed through the speakers. She assured her fellow Southerners that her husband had signed the Civil Rights Act to uphold the Constitution for all people, all regions, all states.

"Lyndon has offered to unify this country, to put behind us things of the past," she said.

As folks listened, Lady Bird noticed protest signs coming down and a few nods of agreement.

With one successful speech behind her, Lady Bird looked forward to hosting city, state, and federal representatives on board as part of the campaign. Within the Special's two dining cars, she offered authentic Southern food such as hush puppies, grits, and black-eyed peas.

Time to roll on down the line to
five more station stops, five more
speeches, five more receptions before
leaving Virginia and the cities for "land where
the pavement runs out and city people don't often go."

One such place was **AHOSKIE, NORTH CAROLINA**, a town much like Lady Bird's childhood home, with its open farmland, church steeples, and general store.

During the stop, a woman approached Lady Bird, shook her hand, and said, "I got up at three o'clock this morning and milked twenty cows so I could get here by train time!"

Perhaps Lady Bird remembered the loneliness of rural life when she replied: "I am glad we met and touched."

Lady Bird now hoped LBJ's message could reach every nook and cranny in the South. Six more stops before nightfall. . . .

On the second day, the train whooshed through rugged North Carolina and into **SOUTH CAROLINA**, where real trouble brewed.

In **COLUMBIA**, the crowd's grumbling erupted into shouting. Groups of young men interrupted Lady Bird's speech with loud chants of "We Want Barry" (Barry Goldwater—LBJ's political opponent). Hecklers held up signs.

Lady Bird stood strong; she would not be rattled by protestors.

She only gestured *stop*, holding out her hand. Speaking over the noise, Lady Bird announced, "This is a country of many viewpoints. I respect your right to express your own. Now it is my turn to express mine. Thank you."

To the surprise of all, the crowd hushed.

Lady Bird continued her message. "My husband not only talks of peace, but works for peace. . . ."

On to **CHARLESTON**, the last event of the day. As a former port for the slave trade, Charleston had a history of unequal treatment of Blacks that dated back longer than most Southern cities. Lady Bird expected resistance to her visit.

The local newspaper, also afraid that spectators might be rude to the First Lady, asked citizens to show courtesy.

Despite this plea, protesters never stopped booing. But in response, Lady Bird addressed her fellow citizens as "my friends," asking them to welcome desegregation, prosperity, and peaceful communities for a better future.

An exhausted Lady Bird hoped to catch a few winks
before the next day's seven scheduled station stops,
seven speeches, seven receptions. . . .

On the third day, the train moved deeper into the South, and demonstrators grew bolder.

In **SAVANNAH, GEORGIA**, protestors taunted Lady Bird, cursed her family, and carried signs.

But not even rumors of snipers stopped Lady Bird from reaching out to her people. After stating "I have a mighty happy feeling to see y'all out there," she walked down the train platform steps, shook the hands of well-wishers, and even spoke face-to-face with protestors.

Back on board for a few more stops, the Special then headed out to reach DRIFTON and TALLAHASSEE, FLORIDA, before nightfall.

But the Secret Service had received an anonymous bomb threat: an upcoming seven-mile bridge might be the perfect place for hidden explosives. To keep the First Lady safe, the Secret Service sprang into action under cover of night, sweeping the bridge for dynamite and other devices. They found no bombs, but at dawn they sent a decoy train across the bridge. Lady Bird worried only about the engineer and conductor steering the decoy, not her own safety.

When the Special itself crossed the tracks, a helicopter hovered overhead. Several boats, with federal officers aboard, stood ready beneath the bridge.

Not even a bomb threat stopped Lady Bird from rollin' on down the line.

On the fourth and final day, all stops in Florida behind her, Lady Bird's mood lightened as she reached **ALABAMA**. As the home of her extended family, she welcomed her cousins, inviting them to pile on board at each stop. Lady Bird told the **MOBILE** crowd: ". . . I declare if I didn't see two more [cousins] and we stopped and brought them in with us, too."

As the train rolled through **MISSISSIPPI**, folks parked alongside the tracks in many remote areas just to catch a glimpse.

Lady Bird delivered her most confident speech in **BILOXI**, certain in what she had to say. Above the protests, she told the crowd she believed they would choose and vote wisely in the upcoming November election.

The train finally arrived in **NEW ORLEANS, LOUISIANA**, the last stop of the tour.

Thousands of cheering people welcomed Lady Bird at the station—Black and White—happy for her success.

Bands played;

cameras snapped;

newsmen reported.

Lady Bird burst into tears at the warm reception, wiping them away before speaking. At the podium, she gave her last speech of the tour, then said her goodbyes and thank-yous to the Southern crowd.

After traveling more than 1,600 miles and speaking to nearly half a million Southerners, the first solo campaign by a First Lady came to an end.

In her later years, Lady Bird remembered the tour fondly, writing: "I wouldn't take anything for the Whistle-Stop through the South—47 stops in 4 days . . . that very special time, those four most dramatic days in my political life."

Lady Bird Special

Each of the Special's 19 train cars served a purpose (sleeping, dining, press). The last car, freshly painted red, white, and blue and decorated with streamers and flags, served as the campaign car. Personally selected by President Johnson, this unique car held a brass-plated platform for speeches and an open interior for receiving guests.

The Special carried not only Lady Bird and her daughters, Lynda and Luci, but also 150 media members, 15 official hostesses, hundreds of congressmen, and dozens of President Johnson's staff (including the Secret Service).

Not everyone in the gathered crowds wanted to protest. Supporters wishing Lady Bird well brought all sorts of gifts—flowers, bags of peanuts, pies, and jars of jelly. Even Alabama's strongest supporter of segregation, Governor George Wallace, sent roses. Lady Bird gave most of the gifts to children's group homes, elderly facilities, or hospitals.

Lady Bird left campaign gifts all along the Whistle-Stop's route:
- ★ 30,000 plastic train whistles
- ★ 24,000 paper engineer hats
- ★ 160 cases of saltwater taffy
- ★ 6,000 ladies' straw hats with *LBJ* stitched into the rim
- ★ 100,000 postcards with a stamp reading: *Sent from the Lady Bird Special*

★ WHISTLE-STOP TIMELINE ★

*Unscheduled slowdown—unexpected crowds, either parked along railways near the stop or waiting at the station   **Unscheduled stop—enormous crowds at actual station

DAY ONE: OCTOBER 6, 1964
- ★ Washington, DC (train departs from station)
- ★ Alexandria, Virginia (Lady Bird send-off)
- ★ Fredericksburg, Virginia (first scheduled stop)
- ★ Ashland, Virginia
- ★ Richmond, Virginia
- ★ Petersburg, Virginia
- ★ Suffolk, Virginia
- ★ Norfolk, Virginia
- ★ Ahoskie, North Carolina
- ★ Hobgood, North Carolina*
- ★ Tarboro, North Carolina
- ★ Rocky Mount, North Carolina
- ★ Wilson, North Carolina
- ★ Selma, North Carolina
- ★ Raleigh, North Carolina

DAY TWO: OCTOBER 7, 1964
- ★ Durham, North Carolina
- ★ Burlington, North Carolina**
- ★ Greensboro, North Carolina
- ★ High Point, North Carolina**
- ★ Thomasville, North Carolina
- ★ Lexington, North Carolina
- ★ Salisbury, North Carolina
- ★ Concord, North Carolina
- ★ Charlotte, North Carolina
- ★ Rock Hill, South Carolina
- ★ Chester, South Carolina
- ★ Winnsboro, South Carolina
- ★ Columbia, South Carolina
- ★ Orangeburg, South Carolina
- ★ Charleston, South Carolina

DAY THREE: OCTOBER 8, 1964
- ★ Ravenel, South Carolina*
- ★ Green Pond, South Carolina*
- ★ Yemassee, South Carolina*
- ★ Ridgeland, South Carolina**
- ★ Savannah, Georgia
- ★ Jesup, Georgia
- ★ Blackshear, Georgia**
- ★ Waycross, Georgia
- ★ Homerville, Georgia**
- ★ Valdosta, Georgia
- ★ Thomasville, Georgia
- ★ Drifton, Florida
- ★ Tallahassee, Florida

DAY FOUR: OCTOBER 9, 1964
- ★ Chattahoochee, Florida
- ★ Chipley, Florida
- ★ Crestview, Florida
- ★ Pensacola, Florida
- ★ Flomaton, Alabama
- ★ Mobile, Alabama
- ★ Biloxi, Mississippi
- ★ New Orleans, Louisiana (end of tour)

Lyndon Johnson won the 1964 presidential election by a landslide. Three Southern states—Virginia, North Carolina, and Florida—not expected to support President Johnson, voted to re-elect the president. Lady Bird's show of grit, grace, and courtesy toward her fellow Southerners likely changed these voters' minds.

Lady Bird Johnson reads to a group of Head Start children. March, 1968

Lady Bird Johnson was born on December 22, 1912, and officially named Claudia Alta Taylor. It's not clear how the nickname Lady Bird stuck. Some sources say it was her caretaker, Alice Tittle, and others believe the credit goes to her childhood friends.

The First Lady is perhaps best remembered as championing the Highway Beautification Act of 1965, nicknamed Lady Bird's Bill. After the act passed, Lady Bird worked tirelessly with the states to plant wildflowers along our nation's highways; her work was also crucial to the passing of the Wild and Scenic Rivers Act of 1968. In addition, she encouraged the passing

BIBLIOGRAPHY

"Lady Bird Johnson," (PBS website), 2001, accessed March 1, 2017.

Gillette, Michael L. *Lady Bird Johnson: An Oral History*. Oxford University Press, 2012.

Hindley, Meredith. "Lady Bird Special: Mrs. Johnson's Southern Strategy." *Humanities*, Vol. 34, No. 3.

Johnson, Claudia Alta. *Lady Bird Johnson: A White House Diary*. Holt, Rinehart & Winston, 1970.

Russell, Jan Jarboe. *Lady Bird: A Biography of Mrs. Johnson*. Scribner, 1999.

Temple, Louann Atkins. *Lady Bird Johnson: Deeds Not Words*. Dog Ear Publishing, 2013.

SOURCE NOTES

"This isn't right . . ." *Lady Bird: A Biography of Mrs. Johnson*, (Scribner, 1999), p. 52.

"as much a part of the South . . ." *Lady Bird: A Biography of Mrs. Johnson*, (Scribner, 1999), p. 257.

"deeds, not words," *Lady Bird Johnson: Deeds Not Words*, (Dog Ear Publishing, 2013), p. 35.

"Sunshine and lots of friends . . ." *Lady Bird: A Biography of Mrs. Johnson*, (Scribner, 1999), p. 253.

". . . look for the ties . . ." Lady Bird Special: Mrs. Johnson's Southern Strategy." *Humanities*. Vol. 34, No. 3, 2013, n. p.

"Lyndon has offered . . ." *Lady Bird: A Biography of Mrs. Johnson*, (Scribner, 1999), p. 253.

"land where the pavement runs out . . ." *Lady Bird: A Biography of Mrs. Johnson*, (Scribner, 1999), p. 256.

of legislation creating Head Start, an early-childhood literacy initiative that helped prepare impoverished children to be successful students before they began kindergarten.

However, it is Lady Bird's little-known Whistle-Stop Tour that highlights her strength and determination. Her good friend, reporter Bill Moyers, accompanied her as a White House special assistant. He witnessed her bravery and resolve in the face of hecklers and threats, astonished that she ignored her own safety.

Lady Bird Johnson standing at the rear of the White House, 1960.

Moyers reminded the world in Lady Bird's eulogy that she never backed down from her beliefs and principles. No matter how others acted toward her, she always reached for the "beauty in democracy . . . the beauty in us."

"I got up at three o'clock . . ." *A White House Diary,* (Holt, Rinehart & Winston, 1970), p. 199.

"I am glad we met . . ." *A White House Diary,* (Holt, Rinehart & Winston, 1970), p. 199.

"This is a country . . ." *Lady Bird: A Biography of Mrs. Johnson,* (Scribner, 1999), p. 258.

"My husband not only . . ." The LBJ Library (2014, October 5), Lady Bird's Whistle Stop: Columbia, SC: 10/7/64, 3:58 p.m.

"I have a mighty happy feeling . . ." The LBJ Library (2014, October 7), Lady Bird's Whistle Stop: Savannah, GA: 10/8/64, 11:50 a.m.

"I declare if I didn't . . ." The LBJ Library (2014, October 7), Lady Bird's Whistle Stop: Mobile, AL: 10/9/64, 2:36 p.m.

"I wouldn't take anything . . ." *A White House Diary,* (Holt, Rinehart & Winston, 1970), p. 198.

"beauty in democracy . . . the beauty in us." Bill Moyers eulogy for Lady Bird Johnson. 14 July 2007, Austin, Texas. (C-SPAN, 2007)

PHOTOS:
Page 36: LBJ Presidential Library
Page 38: National Parks Gallery, https://npgallery.nps.gov/
Page 39: National First Ladies Library & Museum

For Eva—my sister, my friend
—HK

For Faith Marie—my daughter, my brave one
—RL

In memory of Robert and Louise McInnis
—Erin

SLEEPING BEAR PRESS™

2395 South Huron Parkway, Suite 200, Ann Arbor, MI 48104
www.sleepingbearpress.com © Sleeping Bear Press

Printed and bound in the United States
10 9 8 7 6 5 4 3 2 1

Library of Congress Cataloging-in-Publication Data
Names: Kampion, Helen, author. | Lyons, Reneé Critcher, 1961- author. | McGuire, Erin, illustrator.
Title: Rollin' on down the line : Lady Bird Johnson's 1964 whistle-stop tour for civil rights /
written by Helen Kampion and Reneé Critcher Lyons ; illustrated by Erin McGuire.
Other titles: Rolling on down the line | Description: Ann Arbor, MI : Sleeping Bear Press, [2024] | Includes
bibliographical references. | Audience: Ages 6-10 | Summary: "The true story of First Lady "Lady Bird" Johnson's historic 1964 Whistle-Stop
train journey, making almost fifty stops through eight Southern states in four days to campaign on behalf of her husband's reelection in the
wake of the signing of the Civil Rights Act"-- Provided by publisher. | Identifiers: LCCN 2024005250 | ISBN 9781534113015
Subjects: LCSH: Presidents--United States--Election--1964--Juvenile literature. | Johnson, Lady Bird, 1912-2007--Juvenile literature. |
Johnson, Lyndon B. (Lyndon Baines), 1908-1973--Juvenile literature. | Presidents' spouses--United States--Juvenile literature. | African
Americans--Civil rights--History--20th century--Juvenile literature. | United States--Politics and government--1963-1969--Juvenile literature.
Classification: LCC E850 .K36 2024 | DDC 973.923--dc23/eng/20240220 | LC record available at https://lccn.loc.gov/2024005250